Ebony Locks
AND THE
Star Apple Tree

Written By
Glasmine Scully

Illustrated by
Kedar "ArtbyAncient" Davis

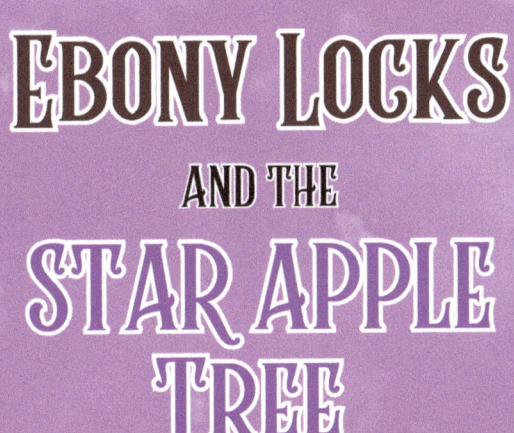

Ebony Locks and the Star Apple Tree
Text and illustration copyright © 2024 by Glasmine Scully

All rights reserved.
No part of this publication may be reproduced, distributed, or transmitted in any form or by any means, including photocopying, recording, or other electronic or mechanical methods, without the prior written permission of the publisher, except as permitted by copyright law.

First Edition 2024

ISBN
Paperback 978-1-998245-10-9
Hardcover 978-1-998245-11-6

Book design by Kabrena L. Robinson
Published by Eva-Michelle & Family Publishing
www.evamichelleandfamily.com

Dedicated to

My daughter Imani, for your positive vibes throughout the creation of this story.

Special Thanks

To Ms. Gail, for your inspiring support and unwavering belief in my writing abilities.

To Ms. Shawna, your assistance and encouragement were instrumental in initiating and completing my story.

CONTENTS

Chapter 1..............................p. 2

Chapter 2..............................p. 10

Chapter 3..............................p. 16

Chapter 4..............................p. 29

Chapter 5..............................p. 40

Glossary

Chapter 1

A long time ago on the island of Jamaica, there lived a curious little girl named Ebony Locks.

Ebony lived with her grandmother in an old gray house on top of a hill in Mango Grove, a town in the parish of St. Elizabeth.

She would spend most of her days exploring the grounds surrounding her house. She observed the many plants, animals, and insects around her.

She could often be found crouched over an ant's nest curiously watching the tiny creatures move to and from, taking leaves, twigs, and fruits to their nest.

The different things she observed sparked her interest and imagination.

The house was surrounded by all kinds of delicious fruits and vegetables–like juicy mangoes, guavas, sweetsops and papayas.

Ebony's favorite fruit to eat was the star apple. She would dream all day about sinking her teeth into a ripe star apple. She loved how it was purple on the outside and white, sweet, and pulpy on the inside.

The sweetest star apples were found deep in the forest below the hill where her gray house stood.

Ebony's grandmother would always warn her to never venture into the forest by herself. Her grandmother feared that Ebony would find herself lost and alone.

"Yuh too likkle to be wandering off into di forest by yuh self," her grandma would often warn her.

·····

One sunny afternoon, Ebony and her grandmother were sitting on their verandah. Ebony was reading her favourite Brer Anansi storybook, while her grandmother sat in her old rocking chair reading the newspaper.

Ebony's grandmother would always read her newspaper.

"You have to know what's going on in the country," she would always preach to Ebony.

After a couple of minutes, Ebony heard her grandmother snoring and leaned over to see if she was sleeping.

She was fast asleep, still holding on tightly to her newspaper.

Ebony started to think about all the adventures she could go on while her grandmother took her afternoon nap.

She thought about milking the cows on her own. She thought about making a kite to fly down the hill. She thought about climbing the East Indian mango tree at the front of the yard to reach the ripest mangoes at the top.

Then, she started to daydream about the star apples deep in the forest.

"I could go into the forest to fetch a couple and be back before grandma wakes up," she thought to herself.

Ebony sneaked past her grandmother, slipped into her favourite red sandals and grabbed her grandmother's bankra basket.

She was determined to find those star apples. Ebony Locks set out on her journey toward the forest.

Chapter 2

The sun was shining brightly outside. Ebony felt the sun's warmth on her chocolate-brown glowing skin.

She felt brave. She didn't mind going alone. She thought about the sweet smell of the star apples and the gooey sweet liquid oozing out over her hands and mouth as she ate.

She was determined to find the star apple trees.

She thought about all the things she would encounter as she walked through the forest.

She was eager and excited.

As she walked down the hill, a strong wind forced her to the bottom. Ebony Locks paused for a moment, trying to decide which way to go.

"Where are the star apple trees, I wonder?" She said as she tilted her head toward the sun.

"Mr. Sun, which way shall I go? Shall I go here, or shall I go there? Please tell me if you know."

She decided to walk slowly to the left of the track between the forest of swaying trees.

Ebony felt the warm breeze blowing through her thick, curly locks. Her hair blew in all directions like the swaying trees. She felt as free as the wind.

Flip, flop, flip, flop, went her slippers as the sound echoed through the air in the silent forest.

On her way, she admired all kinds of wildflowers. She stopped to pick a couple of wild hog plums and passion fruits. She picked three passion fruits, cracked the shells open, and gobbled up the sweet jelly-like fruit inside.

Afterwards, she walked for about three miles, looking left and right for the star apple trees.

After some time, she realized that she was lost. Ebony stood and looked around.

"I must have taken the wrong path," she began to worry. She was confused but she kept on walking.

"I must find those star apple trees!"

Chapter 3

After walking for some time, she came upon a big yard surrounded by a wooden fence.

"I wonder who lives here," she thought as she wandered around curiously.

The yard had three buildings. There was an old outdoor kitchen, a latrine, and the main house.

"I am so thirsty from all that walking. Maybe someone will give me a drink of water, then I will go and find the star apple trees," Ebony Locks said out loud to herself.

She walked up to the kitchen made of wood with a palm thatch roof. She peeped through the spaces between the wooden frame of the door, but there was no one inside.

"I wonder what kind of food I will find in this kitchen?" She wondered.

She could hear her tummy rumbling. She entered the kitchen and looked around.

On the counter, there were three enamel plates with three forks next to each of them. There was a large, medium and small plate.

She thought for a moment then took up the small plate, there were three slices of roasted yellow heart breadfruit with ackee and saltfish on the side.

Ebony Locks licked her lips and then pinched a little piece of creamy yellow-heart breadfruit.

It was delicious, it melted in her mouth. She decided to try another piece, this time with some ackee and saltfish.

"This is so tasty!" She exclaimed as she ate.

She could not stop herself, before she knew it, all the breadfruit and ackee and saltfish were gone from the small plate.

After eating she felt thirsty. She started to search around the kitchen for something to drink.

She spotted three mugs on the counter–a small, medium and large sized one.

She decided to choose the medium size mug this time. Ebony picked up the medium-sized mug and saw that it was filled with lemonade. She gulped it all down.
"Ahhh! Refreshing!"
she exclaimed.

After eating the delicious breadfruit with ackee and saltfish and drinking the refreshing lemonade, she thought to herself, "Some sweet juicy star apples would be the perfect treat right now."

She started to wander around the yard again hoping she would find a star apple tree.

She came to the front of the main house and noticed that the door was unlocked. She peeped through the crack of the door and saw that the house was empty.

She decided to take a quick look inside before continuing her quest to find a star apple tree.

The door creaked as she pushed it open and went inside. In the corner of the living room was a big gramophone. Ebony approached it with amazement.

She had never seen one before. She was used to listening to music only on the old antenna radio her grandmother would play.

Ebony curiously sifted through the records on the floor next to the gramophone.

She found one of her favourite songs that her grandmother would always sing.

Guh dung a Manuel Road,
Galang bwoy, fi go bruck rock-stone.
Bruk dem one by one (galang bwoy)
Bruk dem two by two (galang bwoy)
Bruk dem three by three (galang bwoy)
Bruk dem four by four (galang bwoy)
Finger mash nuh cry (galang bwoy!)
Memba a play we dah play (galang bwoy!)

Everything else was forgotten. The beat caught her feet, and she began to dance! As soon as the recording stopped, she played it again and again, inventing new moves each time.

After dancing for a while, she remembered she had yet to find any star apples.

There was a door in the main house that led to the backyard. Ebony headed through the door and stepped outside.

She noticed that the sun was close to setting, she had been gone for a while and her grandmother would have woken up from her nap by now.

She thought about heading home but she was determined to find her star apples.

She looked around the backyard and to her surprise, right in front of her stood the biggest star apple tree she had ever seen.

The star apples were purple and full. Ebony was filled with delight as she looked up at the tree with the biggest smile on her face.

Underneath the tree was an old bucket filled with freshly picked star apples.

She ran to fill her basket and sat down under the tree to taste one... then two... then three...

Soon, she had eaten so many star apples

she had a stomachache. She sat under the tree feeling sick and sleepy. Before she knew it, she dozed off into a deep sleep.

Chapter 4

While Ebony Locks was fast asleep under the star apple tree, the family that lived at the house came home.

They had an exhausting day in the capital town, Black River. Aunt Kizzi, Uncle Ekon, and Nia, their niece, had gone to sell their produce in the market.

As soon as they arrived home, Uncle Ekon lifted Nia from the donkey and tied it to a tamarind tree. Aunt Kizzi took the basket from the top of her head and put it away.

They washed their hands over the cistern as the cool water ran down from the standpipe and soothed their tired hands.

"I am so hungry! I cannot wait to eat," said Nia.

"I am hungry too," said Uncle Ekon. "Nia, you and Aunt Kizzi can sit down while I warm the food."

Nia eagerly ran to the kitchen and sat down on her little bench. She took her plate up to peek at the delicious food.

"Look here! she shouted. "My dish is empty, all the food is gone!" "Somebody must have eaten it!" Nia shouted, looking sad.

Aunt Kizzi and Uncle Ekon quickly took up their plates to take a look but their food was not touched.

"Don't be sad, Nia," said Uncle Ekon, "We will share our food with you."

The food was so enjoyable that their plates were empty in no time. After eating, they decided to drink their lemonade.

Aunt Kizzy handed Uncle Ekon and Nia their mugs. They both thanked her and waited for her to sit down.

Aunt Kizzy reached for her mug, but it came up lightly in her hand. She could not believe what was happening.

Aunt Kizzy turned the cup upside down. "Look!" she gasped, "all my lemonade is gone, now my cup is empty!"

Although no one knew why part of their meal had disappeared, Nia calmly said, "Don't worry Aunt Kizzy, now it is our turn to share with you."

Uncle Ekon lined up the three mugs and poured some of his and Nia's lemonade into Aunt Kizzy's mug. They drank, enjoying every bit of the tangy liquid.

"This is so refreshing," said Nia.

After dinner, they sat on their benches and talked for a while. Uncle Ekon spoke about their African heritage.

"We are the descendants of proud people from the Akan tribe of Ghana, who spoke a language called Twi," he bellowed proudly.

As usual, Nia listened intently, hanging on to her uncle's every word.

She always felt a deep sense of pride when Uncle Ekon talked about how wise and strong their ancestors were.

She especially liked to hear about her great-grandfather, Kojo, a maroon, who along with others fought for their freedom.

"Grandpa Kojo worked hard, saved his money, and bought this piece of land that we are now living on," he explained.

After listening to Uncle Ekon's stories they decided to head to the main house to get ready for bed.

As they approached the house, they saw a pair of tiny red sandals in front of the door. Nia clutched her aunt's hand tightly as they pushed the door open.

They wondered who it belonged to. After looking around, they saw that the house was empty. Uncle Ekon noticed that the needle on his gramophone was still spinning.

"This is strange!" He exclaimed. "Strange things are happening this evening," said Uncle Ekon while he turned off the gramophone.

Nia was still scared, so she gripped her aunt's hand tighter and walked slowly as they continued to search the house. Aunt Kizzy and Nia decided to check the backyard.

•••••

Ebony Locks was in deep sleep, but she heard the voices around her.

When she opened her eyes, she saw three confused faces looking down at her.

She was so frightened that she could hear her heart pounding through her chest.

She quickly sprang to her feet. Her first thought was to run away, but her body could not move, and she was shaking with fear.

The three people stared with worried looks on their faces.

"What is your name, and how did you get here?" shouted Nia, who was no longer scared.

Ebony was still frightened, but she mumbled her name and told them that she had gotten lost on her way to pick some star apples

She apologized for eating their food, drinking their lemonade and almost eating all the star apples they had picked.

"Aren't you the little girl who lives up the hill with your grandmother?" interrupted Aunt Kizzy.

"Yes Ma'am," replied Ebony, timidly.

"Does your grandmother know that you are wandering off on your own?" asked Aunt Kizzy.

Ebony Locks hung her head while playing with her fingers. She finally found the courage to speak to Aunt Kizzy.

"Grandma fell asleep, and I just wanted to explore on my own and find some star apples," she replied.

Aunt Kizzy gave her a stern warning, the same warning that her grandmother would give her about going off into the forest alone.

"Well, this is all over now," Uncle Ekon chimed in. "It is getting late, let's get you home. I know your grandmother must be worried."

Aunt Kizzy packed a basket with all kinds of fruits. She packed some tamarinds, sweetsops, ripe bananas and oranges. She also filled Ebony's bankra basket with all the star apples she could eat.

It was sunset, the air was cool, the trees were still, and the birds chirped their sweet songs.

Nia and Ebony skipped along the path while Uncle Ekon carried the baskets and talked with Aunt Kizzy.

They walked through the forest until they got to the bottom of the hill. Uncle Ekon and Ebony waved goodbye to Aunt Kizzy and Nia as they went ahead up the hill toward the gray house.

Chapter 5

Meanwhile, Ebony's grandmother had been searching for her everywhere.

When she woke up from her afternoon nap and did not see Ebony, at first, she thought that she was playing in the backyard with the goats, but she was not there.

Her grandmother checked the cows' pen—she had warned Ebony not to try milking the cows by herself.

Her grandmother looked and looked, but Ebony was nowhere to be found.

Her grandmother had become worried, so she hastily got dressed in her bandana market dress.

She set out to search the district for Ebony. She searched everywhere but she could not find her.

Feeling sad and worried she came home and sat on the verandah in her old rocking chair. She waited and hoped that Ebony would come home.

The sun was beginning to set and just as she was about to lose hope, she saw two people from afar walking up the hill. She sprung up from her chair and looked over the balcony.

It was Ebony and Uncle Ekon from the little cottage in the forest. Her grandmother dashed off the verandah and ran to greet them.

Ebony ran straight into her grandmother's arms and held her tightly. They both hugged for a while as if they had not seen each other for a long time.

Ebony then told her grandmother all about her little adventure into the forest and how she got lost and apologized for sneaking off while she was asleep.

Grandma wanted to scold Ebony but was so happy that she had returned home.

"Yuh almost give yuh granny a heart attack, next time yuh must listen to what I tell yuh," her grandmother said in a loving but stern tone.

Her grandmother thanked Uncle Ekon for bringing Ebony home safely. Uncle Ekon handed them the baskets of fruits waved goodbye and set off.

Grandma and Ebony Locks sat down on the steps of their verandah.

Ebony shared all the details of her adventure with her and they both had a good laugh about it all.

They sat and watched the sun as it was setting from the top of the hill.

Grandma reached into the basket for one of the star apples. As she took a bite she leaned over and smiled at Ebony.

"Well, at least yuh likkle adventure was worth it. These star apples are real sweet chile."

Ebony Locks chuckled as she grabbed a star apple for herself. As she sank her teeth into the juicy pulpy fruit, she thought about the day and everything that happened.

She made new friends too. From that day, Aunt Kizzy, Uncle Ekon and Nia would regularly visit, bringing all the star apples Ebony could eat.

Ebony was happy to be home with her grandmother and she learnt an important lesson. She never wandered off into the forest alone again.

GLOSSARY

Jamaica

Jamaica is a vibrant and colorful island located in the Caribbean Sea.

©Getty Images via Canva.com

©Uncommon Caribbean

Jamaica is a tropical paradise with glowing sunshine, beautiful beaches, lush green mountains, and tropical forests.

It is home to exotic plants and animals, including the national bird, Doctor Bird, also known as the Hummingbird.

The island is famous for its reggae music and tasty food, including jerk chicken, patties, ackee and saltfish - their national dish, and roasted breadfruit.

©Getty Images via Canva.com

Jamaica is a place of warmth, laughter, and adventure, where the sunsets are stunning, and every day feels like a celebration!

Starapple

©Getty Images via Canva.com

The star apple, known as "cainito", is a tropical fruit that is as delightful to the eyes as it is to the taste buds. This round, green or purple fruit gets its name from the star-shaped pattern visible when it is sliced open. Inside, you will find a sweet and juicy pulp with a unique flavor, often described as a blend of apple and pear, making it a delicious and refreshing treat on a warm Jamaican day.

Brer Anansi

©Kabrena Robinson

Anansi is an Akan folktale character associated with stories, wisdom, knowledge, and trickery, most commonly depicted as a spider in Akan folklore. Taking the role of a trickster, he is also one of the most important characters of West African, African American, and West Indian folklore. Originating in Ghana, these spider tales were transmitted to the Caribbean by way of the transatlantic slave trade.

Bankra Basket

©Getty Images via Canva.com

The "bankra" basket is a traditional Jamaican basket skillfully woven from local materials like straw or bamboo. It features unique patterns and designs, with a sturdy handle for easy carrying. Passed down through generations of Afro-Jamaicans, the weaving techniques add authenticity and make it a symbol of Jamaican heritage and an eco-friendly accessory.

Palm Thatch Roof

©Getty Images via Canva.com

A palm thatch roof is a traditional roofing style that uses materials from palm trees to create a natural and environmentally friendly covering for homes or structures.

Latrine

©Farm Up Jamaica

In the past, Jamaica's sanitation infrastructure was not as developed as it is today, and latrines were used for waste disposal. Pit latrines were common in rural settings, while basic or communal latrines were prevalent in urban areas, especially in informal settlements.

Passion Fruit

©Health Jade via Canva.com

The passion fruit is an exotic and flavourful fruit that grows in tropical regions, including Jamaica. These small, round fruits have a tough outer rind that may be purple, yellow, or red when ripe. Inside, the pulp is juicy and filled with aromatic, sweet-tart seeds.

Wild Hog Plum

©Alamy via Canva.com

Spondias mombin, commonly known as the Wild Hog Plum, Governor Plum, Jujube, and Spanish Plum, is a fruit with a sweet and tangy flavor. It is often eaten when green and ripe, giving a delightful balance of tartness and sweetness.

Tamarind

©Alamy via Canva.com

The tamarind fruit (Tamarindus indica) is a tropical fruit native to Africa, but commonly found in the Caribbean and South Asia. The tamarind fruit is found inside a hard, brown pod that resembles a large, elongated bean. It has a unique taste that is sweet, tangy, and slightly sour.

Breadfruit

©Getty Images via Canva.com

Breadfruit is a starchy tropical fruit that is a staple in Jamaican cuisine. It is native to the South Pacific but was introduced to Jamaica and other Caribbean islands in the late 18th century. It has a green bumpy outer skin and dense cream-coloured or yellowish flesh. Breadfruit can be cooked in various ways, including roasting, boiling, frying, or even baking. It has a texture similar to bread when cooked, which is how it got its name.

Ackee and Saltfish

©Chris De La Rosa

Ackee and saltfish are the main ingredients of the national dish of Jamaica. Ackee, a tropical fruit native to West Africa, was brought to the Caribbean during the transatlantic slave trade. Salted cod was introduced to Jamaica by the British, who colonised the island. The combination of ackee and saltfish reflects the fusion of African, Caribbean, and European culinary traditions.

Gramophone

Public Domain

A gramophone, also known as a phonograph, is an early sound-reproducing device that was widely used for playing recorded sound during the late 19th and early 20th centuries.

Standpipe/Cistern

©National Storage Tank

The "standpipe," known to some Jamaicans as the "ceston" or cistern, is a pipe located outside the house, typically in the backyard, equipped with a makeshift or well-constructed container for storing and draining water. The term "ceston" or "cistern" dates back to a time when cisterns were commonly used before the advent of more advanced and easily accessible water supply systems.

Bandana

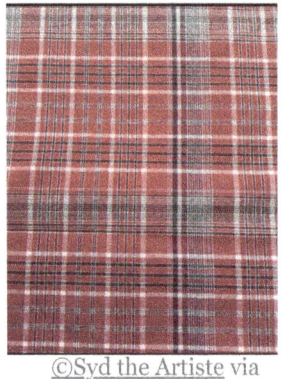
©Syd the Artiste via Pintrest.com

Bandana cloth, historically used to make clothing for enslaved and Black working-class women in the Caribbean, is now a symbol of pride and distinction for Jamaicans. It's lightweight, durable, and worn during ceremonial, cultural, and independence holidays. It is known as the Jamaican National Costume.

Akan Tribe

Wikipedia/ Public Domain

The Twi people are an Akan ethnic group native to Ghana in West Africa. During the era of the transatlantic slave trade, many Akan people, including those who spoke Twi, were among those captured and transported to the Caribbean, including Jamaica.

The influence of Akan culture, language, and traditions can be found in various aspects of Jamaican culture, particularly in the cultural practices, folklore, and language of the Jamaican Maroons.

The Maroons

Image by Sunshine and Stilettos

The Maroons were communities of escaped enslaved Africans who established independent societies in the mountainous regions of Jamaica. They maintained some aspects of their African heritage, including elements of Akan culture. Today, Jamaican Maroon communities continue to celebrate their unique cultural identity.

Photo Attribution
All images used in this book are either sourced from royalty-free platforms, used with permission, or are original works by the author. Every effort has been made to attribute images appropriately. If any image has been used without proper credit, it is unintentional. Please contact the author for any necessary corrections.

Song Attribution
"Guh Dung A Manuel Road" is a traditional Jamaican folk song often sung by children during stone-passing games that mimic quarry work. It has been passed down orally through generations and remains a cherished part of Jamaica's musical heritage.